Pebbles from the Stream

Pebbles from the Stream

*A Collection of Poems by
the Mad River Poets*

Mad River Poets
Mad River Valley, Vermont
Duxbury, Fayston, Moretown, Waitsfield and Warren

Library of Congress Cataloging-in-Publication Data
811.08
M   Mad River Poets
         Pebbles from the stream/poems by
         Mad River Poets – Waitsfield, VT
         L. Brown & Sons Printing, © 2002
         100 pages
         1. Title

ISBN 0-9723262-0-0

Cover design: Dorothy Warren
Cover photograph: Carol Johnson Collins
Managing Editor: Earline Marsh

Printed in the United States of America
L. Brown & Sons Printing, Inc.
14-20 Jefferson Street
Barre, Vermont 05641

ACKNOWLEDGMENTS

The Mad River Poets are grateful to Betty Howlett at the Joslin Memorial Library in Waitsfield, where we met regularly to exchange opinions about our poetry and to plan our book.

Larry Brown, our printer, gave generously of his time with valuable suggestions about publishing.

Also helpful in handling the many details of our production were Angela Raycraft and Glee Charlestream at Larry Brown & Sons, Barre.

The following professional writers have given considerable thought to their comments about our work: Francette Cerulli, John Elder, Jean Mellichamp Milliken, Diane Swan, Helen Whybrow, Nancy Means Wright and David Weinstock.

We appreciate Rick Rayfield at The Tempest Book Shop, Waitsfield, along with many friends and relatives who have given us encouragement from the very beginning.

To all these supporters, we express our sincere thanks.

CONTENTS

6

Singing Brook

Carol Johnson Collins

To Seth and Eliza

Illuminated here are moments I am unwilling to forget.
May their light shine on you.
Find pleasure in your writing, comfort in keeping it,
and joy in sharing it.

Also for Mummy
my daily inspiration.

Chores Were Done

Chores were done,
supper was cooking,
and Dad had washed his hands.

He hunched his body
back in the saggy-seated rocker
in the dining room of the brick farmhouse.

He reached over to the cluttered
stand he had built, himself,
and picked up the Marine Band Harmonica.

His arms and hands wrapped
around the instrument,
cupping it, close to his mouth.

He crossed his legs,
and the upper foot began to beat
a rhythm in the air.

His eyes closed, and his brow gathered a bit.
His lips pursed to press
against the open reeds.

A few notes were all I needed,
to know which Irish or Scottish tune
he was in.

I could hear the rocker, rocking,
and feel the rhythm
on the old dining room floor,

to match the rhythm of the tune.

Take Down the Old Fence?

Our sheep dog died.
We sold our sheep.

Now you want to take down
the old sheep fence.

It's all we have left
to remind me of the farm I knew
as a child.

At least
let me remember
the grease on my hands
at shearing time.

Let me remember
the ram who always came
when I called his name.

Let me remember
the lambs jumping
as they played with each other.

Let me remember
holding the newborn lambs
in the spring.

March 30, 2002

Panning for Gold

Riverledge Farm, Grafton, Vermont

Playing at the river after chores was our reward.
I was five years old,
Bobby, age seven, and Cordy, age nine,
were my brothers.
Each of us held an important job.

Cordy was the storyteller.
He was the best one anywhere in the world.
Everything he'd ever seen or heard or read,
he pulled together into rich, detailed stories
about gold prospectors.

This was not a mere stream or brook.
This was a river which
flowed fast, full and free,
carrying endless quantities of gold-filled sand
down to us.

Bobby panned
using an old cake tin,
which Mummy let him take to the river.

Curley, that was me, carefully poured the finest
(almost powdery) sand into jars,
one by one, capping them, sliding them way-back
to the back-most space under the ledge
that stretched itself
over the river
flowing free.

Upon Cutting Seth's Hair

I almost throw it in our woodstove
with other burnables from today, but I stop.

Whose hair is this in my hands?
It is not blond as my own.
It is not black with gray mixed in, as is Fred's.
It is not Eliza's brown with an amber shine.
It is a new shade for our family,
a dark brown on its way to black.
Whose hair is this in my hands?
That of my son, Seth.

Where did the little blond boy go?
He scratched roads and tunnels in the sandbox,
poured water from cup to cup in the bathtub;
he sat for hours making clay figures at the table.

The curls were so blond that people said,
"He looks like an angel child from a Da Vinci painting."
There is no blond in this brown.
Where did the little boy go?

He went to do his homework in French, math and social studies,
and to throw sticks for our dog, Joy,
to read his thick novel,
to build an amazing future vehicle,
to hypothesize about bases and acids and protons.
That's where my little blond boy went!

I wonder if this summer's sun
brings back the little boy in him.

*Given to Seth on his graduation from Johnson State College,
Johnson, Vermont, May 19, 2001*

Mountains of Home

I took a flight to Fort Lauderdale
to attend my cousin's wedding.

Arriving at the fourteen-story luxury hotel,
I stood, staring out the huge windows.

Rain fell endlessly.

All night I tossed and turned
as I heard the drone of trucks
below me on the six-lane highway.

The long hotel hallways, all alike,
floor, after floor, after floor.

The rooms, all alike,
floor, after floor, after floor.

A dead-bolt double-locked
the heavy steel door.

On our last morning,
early,
skies cleared;
a pink sunrise spread across the horizon.

I grabbed my camera.
Squinting through the view-finder,
I found exactly what I wanted to capture!

In the distance, pre-dawn light pink-tinged
the smog-covered skyscrapers.

They looked like the mountains of home.

May 20, 2002

Six Sisters

The final day had come.
Graduation for Alexa, Corinna, Eliza.

Abby came all the way from Boston.

Kirsten made her favorite orange cake.
Each bite brought her family to this circle.

Corinna felt blessed;
her whole family came.

Alexa rolled up her tiny poem-painting
with a ribbon,
a diploma of the heart!

Sherry gave gifts of pottery, a book and hugs.

Being there was everything
and everyone knew it.

Kirsten shouted, *OKAY EVERYBODY,*
LET'S DO A GROUP GOODBYE!
All six women went down to the dock by the little pond.

Smoothly their arms interlaced.
A tight women's circle.
All their heads touched.

Sun flooded the landscape;
the endless spring green became the backdrop
for this permanent pledge.

"Take me there"

"You're not awake yet, Newton;
drink some of your coffee
so that you'll wake up."

Phil came for a quick visit before going to work.
Newton reached to find his son's outstretched hand;
the clasp held for more than a moment.

Later Newton said,
"Phil could have taken me there."

"Where do you want to go?"
Elaine asked.

"Take me downstairs."

"Newton, we aren't up there
at the old house;
we're right here in our kitchen."

"Take me there!" Newton repeated.

"You are right here with me, in our kitchen.
Where do you want to go?"

Newton very clearly replied,

"Take me to where I think I am."

Beside Still Waters

Ann B. Day

For Marian Giles Gleason
(1909-1999)
who still inspires me with her wit and wisdom

Root Beer Water

I remember Punkatasset Pond.
My sisters and I rode our bikes
on hot summer afternoons to swim
in the umber-colored, root beer water.
We could hardly see our legs
as we waded into the pond, and
slimy mud oozed between our toes.
We thought our summer tans
would turn an ugly ocher brown.
Long gray leeches lurked under rocks
and sucked onto our bodies as we swam.

I'm not sure why
we liked to go there;
except it was fun to take
someone there who didn't know
about the strange root beer water,
the oozy mud and sucking leeches,
then watch them scream and jump
and scramble from Punkatasset Pond.

Summer Sanctuary

There is a distant rumble
hardly heard
as we rake hay
in the summer stillness.

A sudden darkening
veils the afternoon sun.
Quickly it comes,
pushing purple-black clouds
over the mountains
and spiraling gray fog
out of the valleys.

We hurry to fork
the last of the load
onto the wagon.
A roar of wind
rattles the hay
and bends the trees.

We reach the barn
just as the first drops
glaze our faces.

The huge loft surrounds us
with sweet, heavy smells of hay
and the rap of rain on the roof.

Ann B. Day

The Quick Coming of Night

The sun descends all too soon
on a late December afternoon.

When we went out to feed the stock,
there'd be a dusk at four o'clock
and the sky would have a purple glow.
Our boots would squeak on frozen snow
when we trod the path our footsteps wore
that threads from kitchen to stable door.

We'd pull the cords of yellow light
to brighten the barn against the night.
The stanchioned cows would moo for grain,
the horses would jangle their tether chain,
the chickens would chortle over their eggs,
the cats would rub against our legs.
We'd feed and milk and hear them chew;
when done we'd leave on a light or two.

I'd see the barn from my kitchen chair
and know it was warm with the animals there.

Now, no lights glow
in the quick coming of night;
snow drifts on the path,
the door of the barn is bolted tight.

Shooting Stars

We sit silently together,
my daughter, her husband-to-be,
my sixteen-year-old son and me,
in the farmhouse kitchen
that overlooks the pasture
where cows graze peacefully.

Frank has gone;
his tormented mind
took him away
in the oppressive heat
and violent storm
of yesterday.

When he did not
come back to do the chores
and milk the cow,
we lay sleepless and chilled
in the blue-black night
dreading the where and the how.

We talked in circles,
words on the phone;
we worried, we cried,
our bodies were stone.
We asked over and over
where and how it could be,

while in the night pasture
the cattle grazed peacefully.

Now we wait in the house,
while the blood hounds bay,
the searchers and police cars
seem far away.

Finally, steps on our porch;
our neighbor and friend
has come to tell us
the where and how of the end.
Near the brook on the hill
in a shaded glade,
Frank took his life
with a carving blade.

The words pass through us
like a plucked brass string;
and now we know
the why is everything.

In the calm of tonight,
we walk up the hill
to watch shooting stars
in the blue-black sky.
"There he goes! He's free!"
says my son and we smile,

while the cows graze peacefully
in the pasture nearby.

July 28, 1970

Boxes

This morning
I found a hen lying
on the dirt floor
of the chicken pen,
her breath coming in heaves.
I picked her up
and placed her on hay
in a cardboard carton
so she could die in peace,
away from the other
cackling hens.

In the afternoon,
a square-sided truck
took away the Highland cows
and a tradition
that has filled these
hillside pastures
for over a hundred years.

I wandered the farmhouse
finding toys, books,
shoes, photo albums,
the doll with a missing eye
and a yellow tea pot.

Now, sitting on packed crates
in the bare-walled kitchen,
lit only by dusk of evening,
I wait for the moving van.

It's hard to put my life,
my heart,
in boxes.

Afternoon Concert

The trio plays
impromptu
in our parlor
while outside October's rain
reminds me of you.

Flute drops
against the yellow leaves,
flat on twigs and trunks
of darkened trees.
Strings slide
down the silver panes,
beyond the puffs
of poplar gold
on hills and wooded lanes.
Piano plays
a beating bass
upon the waters
of the pond
where ripples interlace.

I see your face
as the afternoon of music
mingles rain
and sweet memories
of you,
impromptu.

Confluence

Earline Viola Marsh

Dedicated to my parents
Earl Roland Marsh
who taught me to be a Spartan
and Viola Irene Cheltra Marsh
who taught me about belly-laughs

The Mad River

First gurgle as a mountain rill
   in Granville Gulf,
      the north-flowing Mad
         parts from its south-flowing
      twin, the White.
It curves through steep slopes
   and lends its pathway to Route 100.
      It meanders through
         national historic villages, under
         nineteenth century covered bridges,
   through meadows and gorges,
fueling a lone hydroelectric plant
   and washing the remains of one
      it destroyed in the flood of '27.
Gathering strength from tributaries
   along the way, the Mad is like the
      nursery rhyme girl with a curl –
      very very good or horrid.
A twenty-six mile maverick,
   it shares its name with a
      valley, a watershed,
         commerce, recreation
         and poets.

Black Satin Dress with Pink Ruffles

A tattered box of family mementos
  yields a sepia studio photograph
    of a serene young woman in a black satin dress.
The 1920s look could be Leona or Viola or Cecilia.
  Only Viola, my ninety-three year old mother, survives.
    Visiting her, I ask which sister this is.

"It's Leona," Mom says with a huff in her voice.
  Her platform rocker squeaks more urgently.
    She hands me back the photo.
"I made that black satin dress with
  pink ruffles, the best I ever did; Leona
    wanted it and Ma made me give it to her."

Over the years, I'd heard in the family that Leona was
  the favored first born of nine children; before she
    left home to enter the convent, she was "mean."
In recent years, working on family genealogy, I visited
  Aunt Leona in her small memory-crowded room
    at the Sisters of the Holy Union.

The day after my visit with Mom, at a sixtieth anniversary
  celebration, Aunt Aurore, eighty-five, said to me
    in the ladies' room, "You look so much like Leona."
I'd heard this before, the first time fifteen years ago
  in subdued light at Uncle Don's wake.
    "But you are not like her." Aunt Aurore,
her ash blond curls framing a sweet auntie smile,
  gently patted my shoulder.
    "She was mean."

Private Stock Port

Sioux Lookout train station,
    humiliated by graffiti and boarded windows,
        peels in the early morning sun.
Green long-necked bottles, some smashed to shards,
    with "Private Stock Port" in white letters
        on black labels, litter the trackside.
A few passengers detrain. I follow the lady in a
    lavender suit and tapestry pumps.
VIA Rail's *Canadian* is watered and restocked
    in a twenty minute stop.

First Nations men sit on park benches,
    with quiet talk, bent heads, and brown-bagged bottles.
A lone teenage girl hunches on three concrete steps,
    her ebony hair shining, her face masked from inside.
We do not look at each other as I walk by.

I might have asked her,
    Why are you sitting alone by the railroad tracks
        on a fine Wednesday morning in May?
    What do you think as you look at
        these privileged people on holiday?
    Have you ever ridden the train to elsewhere?

"Board!"
Ian with the flashing white teeth and handsome uniform
    lifts me back into Silver and Blue Luxury Class.
I peer out my window as the train creeps by.
    The three concrete steps are empty.
Men with bent heads still sit on park benches,
    tippling their Private Stock Port.

Driving to Burlington

to interview Jeanne Tourin, January 12, 1998

White-crusted trees hang on ledges
   high above the hydro-dam
      on the Winooski River,
         thundering now with flood waters.
Sunrise filters pink; frozen mists rise
   slow-motion into blue sky
      and float south.

A red and rust pickup truck sits
   abandoned in shallow snow
      crosswise in the I-89 median,
as if parked there while
   its owner is off bird-watching.

Ice storm havoc stills the white city;
   snapped trees crouch in silent after-rage;
      zero-hovering sunshine
         drenches the morning.
Students hunched under backpacks
   breathe out clouds and crunch
      across college quad.

In her sunlit parlor, venerable Jeanne Tourin
   plays with her right hand on the
      stately old Steinway grand piano,
her limp left hand cradled in her lap.
   Music flows from her whole being.

Her photo will be in color on the cover
   of the weekly Country Courier;
      forty old friends will read
   about her, reconnect and
      warm her life.

Scissors and Scarf

Scissors
Burlington Airport

Gasping sobs wracked her small body;
her pink backpack dangled on a reluctant arm.
Her mom, impatient with the scrambled start

of a family trip with three children,
snapped, "We'll get new scissors at Disney World."
Her dad, attempting consolation, said,

"The security lady had to do her job."
The tear-streaked child whimpered,
"But she was so mean."

Scarf
Los Angeles Airport

Behind me in the check-in line stood an imposing man
with a fine mohair scarf – a white-haired contemporary.
Daunted by the stone-faced armed guards,

I ventured, "You must be going to a colder place."
"Yes," he replied, eager too for distraction, "to Salt
Lake City. My son covers Olympic skating for NBC."

The high alert security took time. We talked about
our careers in education, both former principals.
And now? He's a dance host on a cruise ship to Tahiti.

February 5 and 12, 2002

Pajamas

"Your sister Louise really knows how to shop."
Henry, in his threadbare Morris chair,
buttoned up the cashmere cardigan Louise
gave him for his seventy-fifth birthday.
Marie turned away and smiled.
She knew her sister's shopping secret.

Henry's heart condition worsened;
he was confined to his cluttered bedroom
in the white-weathered farmhouse.
Louise bought him a pair of beige silk pajamas.

Later Marie and Louise visited their father;
the bottoms of his pajama legs were
frayed, with dangling threads. Henry said,
>   "These are great pajamas,
>   but the legs were too long.
>   So I cut them off."

Long a frugal farmer,
Henry never knew the truth.
The beige silk pajamas came from the most
exclusive men's shop in Montreal.
As she did with the cashmere sweater,
Louise gave the pajamas to her father
in a blue plastic Wal-Mart bag.

Earline V. Marsh

Today

sense the day
with its elation
and its pain

hug and belly-laugh
bask in the sun
walk in the rain

read a poem
do good work
don't complain

be in the now

Crosscurrents

Carol Milkuhn

Dedicated to
Manfred Milkuhn

Carol Milkuhn

Anne Boleyn's Dressmaker

A dressmaker sees things differently.
Most people remember my lady as wife of a king or mother of a queen,
but I remember that naughty little negligee she wore to Henry's bed –
  black satin drapery I trimmed in orange silk,
  ebony folds flame-frosted, scented with cinnamon and cloves,
  just right for my sophisticated lady,
    who was as feisty and fast-living as the falcon on her crest –
    the kind of woman other women rarely like.

"Raven-haired witch" gossips called her,
citing a blemished fingertip, an extra nail, as proof of Satan's curse.
So I designed a robe with ample sleeves to hide that imperfection –
these jewel-embellished, fox-lined folds are a secret-smothering sheath.

Still, things fall apart, unravel at the end.
Henry enjoyed a romantic chase, but rarely cared for what he caught.
And my lady knew her worth, wouldn't favor, flatter or fawn upon a man –
  the kind of woman some women really like.
  I took care she met death as befits a queen, regally arrayed,
    gowned in rose satin, offset by gray brocade,
      her feet encased in silver slippers, the cutting edge of fashion,
      filigreed and fragile, never meant for walking.

Textile Gallery, Dublin Museum

A museum exhibit now, this Aran sweater,
cabled and coiled by an islander's wife into
a maze of panels and plaits, braids and blackberry knots,
is a blanket of heavy cream promising protection
against the wind-whipped rains of a wintry shore.

Worn by a fisherman risking entombment
under swells of frigid, unforgiving seas,
this knit, a honeycomb of diamonds sculpted in seed stitch,
is frosted by salt-stained, sun-lightened threads,
some fused, felted by frequent washings,
others stretched open, thirsty for life.

Offering

It is the homeless man, dressed in grime-streaked rags,
tugging at my sleeve, who leads me to St. Paul's,
near the World Trade Center, those once proud Twin Towers,
now shards of metal embedded in a mangled earth.
"Music," he mutters,
pointing through misshapen clouds,
through thickened shadows of smoke, and so,

scuffing stone steps worn smooth by centuries,
I enter the church, the oldest in New York. Inside the nave,
even George Washington's pew is piled high with
scarves and socks, sodas and shirts,
with sandwiches from Zabar's and boxes of crumb cake,
Entenmann's scripted in blue on cardboard sides.
Memorials are everywhere: tacked onto walls,

pillars, backs and seats of ancient wooden pews,
a pathway of pictures and poems written on wrappers,
winding down the aisle and outside,
a river of ribbons
flowing to a high iron fence surrounding the church
and to that monstrous concrete crater,
itself wrapped now in forbidding wooden walls.
At noon, there is Eucharist for those who move up front,

past the cots crowding the aisle, past massage therapists who
work on muscles of those who count moments,
firemen and policemen impatient to return,
even to uncover bodies buried in a killing field.
A pianist plays classics on a Steinway grand.
The altar is covered with lilies, paler than I ever recall;
their sticky scent,
        soothing and spirit-stilling,
           allows me to pray.

Awakening

I relax into a padded mat, pulling knees to chest,
and rock, massaging muscles, molding flesh to floor,
while fleece-lined sweats slide smoothly over skin, and I think of

corsets, pantyhose and girdled thighs, of wood and whalebone
creating curves, ample bosoms and hourglass hips,
of being beaded and braided, embroidered and brocaded,
photographed and poured into
        white linen for lawn croquet or
        black satin for afternoon tea,
bell-skirted, bone-waisted, unable to breathe as

I arch my back,
bare feet gripping, body bending to form a bridge,
wondering why women were afraid
of natural, naked and raw,
why I explore my edges only now
that my skin is wrinkled and my hair is turning gray.

Straying

"Don't feed the cat," our landlord warns. But I am sleep-deprived,
            troubled by plaintive mewings and the vocal midnight hauntings
            of this skeletal, black feline who hobbles around the
            blossom-laden garden of our rented Majorcan villa,
                        dragging a withered limb.

And then, shocked, I discover this feral beggar, starvation-crazed,
            licking the soured custard of an éclair, slimy
            ant-covered leftover earmarked for a garbage pail.
            So I smuggle in cat food, tiny tins of tuna and shrimp,
                        rich pickings for a refugee.

"And the landlord?" my husband wonders. But devious now,
            yet compassionate too, I bury telltale cans of
            feline contraband under panty hose and wrinkle creams,
            unwashed laundry and toothpaste tubes, at one with sister Eve
                        who hoped to hide an apple core.

For this is Eden, this island, sun-soaked exotic shore.
            And, as we sip nectar of ripe, freshly squeezed oranges,
            we create mythology,
            embroidering the story of Genesis by adding a stray,
            something unsought, unbidden,
                        for which we risk eviction.

Twenty-One Speed Heaven

This is September and I am going biking
on an abandoned railroad bed of rough-edged cinders,
a tightly packed surface, serpentine and smooth,
a Vermont pathway uncoiling into Canada.
As rural towns fade, lost in my rearview mirror,
as St. Albans melts into meadows, cornstalk-hedged,
we cycle under I-89, a roaring traffic-laden snake
upheld by concrete towers, and into the countryside,
past Holsteins draped in boas of sunshine and shade,
cud-chewing bovines hugging a split rail fence,
past all this and a cherry picker too, until,
hungry and tired, muscles stretched into pain,
taut to the touch, we find a Creemee stand and
eat melted peanut butter over vanilla ice cream.
Then, as the sun etches the mountain ridge golden,
we wait for dusk, paralyzed by a perfect day.

Carol Milkuhn

Walking the Streets of Harlem

feeling warm concrete under my thin-soled shoes
and sun beating on the nape of my neck,
I pass a florist overgrown with a jungle of blossoms,
a promiscuity of roses, exuberance of yellow and red,
a compost of color nurturing new green hopes,
like those dreams of children who tumble
hoop-ready, slam-dunk dizzy,
out of an emptying elementary school
and into
spring, 125th Street style.

Walking the streets of Harlem,
I pass a street musician playing a terrific trombone,
blowing jazz born of blackness and blues, too hot and too cool,
and so, leaning against a lamppost, Crispy Creme in hand,
I throw crumbs to song-starved sparrows and listen
to the off-on rhythm, the finger-snapping beat
of fresh fried fish and silken sun-kissed skin,
sound bytes scooped out of the sky and
scrambled with
spring, 125th Street style.

Images

Ruth Pestle

To my family, friends,
students and teachers

Remembrance

My brother, age seventy-nine,
 and I climb up Pine Hill, passing
  maiden hair, interrupted, Christmas ferns
   and stunted trees where deer have feasted.
    We walk in silence to rock ledges
     overlooking a valley.

He tells me he and Dad came here
  thirty years ago. A doe and her two
   fawns were down below. The fawns
    danced a waltz, then a march
     as their mother called
      the tunes.

As ferns bend slowly in the breeze
 we visitors in transit to eternity
  stand silently, holding fast
   to one last memory of Pine Hill,
    springtime tucked
     into her rock ledges.

Waitsfield Farm

Orvis Jones planned our English-style barn soon after the town
    was founded in 1789. The field stones laid for foundation
    walls were placed exactly sixty by forty feet. Swinging
    his twelve-inch broadax to hew sills twelve by sixty feet,

he married each corner to the next sill's groove. It still
    stands straight, erect. The bark left on beams was no
    hindrance to the barn swallows who built their nests next
    to older ones; falling fledglings became cat food.

Higher, higher went hay pitched off the horse-drawn wagon
    into the bay, then the lofts. I loved jumping up there,
    sneezing, getting dusty and dirty, way up in hay heaven.
    We wintered over two, then three, then nine cows.

Young stock kept in a corner with their own gutter sent spring
    fertilizer to fields. The cycles were milking every twelve
    hours, breeding every year, butchering after seven years
    of milking. Once a year steaks graced Sunday dinner.

Dad's songs wafted through lantern light; cats purred on cows'
    backs; milk foamed in pails. I swung the separator's handle,
    producing skim milk for meals, cream for butter. Sour milk
    went to piglets squealing at the swish in their trough.

Across the road from the barn, our house had smooth stones
    on the cellar floor. Blue Bennington three-gallon crocks
    for packing carrots and beets in leaves sat here; when
    hens molted, other crocks preserved eggs in water glass.

Northern Spy, Macintosh, Winestock and Russet apples
    rested in high bins. In later years shelves glistened with
    canned tomatoes, Kentucky Wonder string beans, bread
    and butter pickles, dill pickles and succotash.

Straight braids of onions and garlic hung from a beam. Mom
    soaked and cooked the dried yellow-eyed beans, making
    some of them into Friday's bean soup; others with maple
    syrup and ginger became Saturday's baked beans.

Sometimes a mousetrap caught a hungry red squirrel;
    other times Dad's keen eye on the .22 sufficed.
    One pesky chipmunk, who had rolled butternuts
    across the roof all fall, slept, its forest planted.

As we put the garden to bed under blankets of leaves,
    the slaughtered pig's bacon and ham were smoked
    using damp corn husks under a barrel. Salt pork
    went into crocks; pickled pig's feet went into jars.

Clouds brought snow – enough to insulate narcissus,
    lily, tulip and snowdrop bulbs – enough for making
    snowmen – but not enough to prevent Dad from
    returning across the road to the barn.

Up in the Attic

I see years of *National Geographic*s, all in order on
    shelves of boards and bricks. No one was permitted
    to cut a picture from them as Dad read aloud to us
    in the evenings about Tibetan monks with saffron
    robes, sultans in desert kingdoms, naked brown babies
    in India always held on their mothers' left hips so
    their right hands were clean for cooking curried rice.

In the corner lies the homemade radio my brother
    used when he put on earphones, "talked" Morse Code
    to friends around the world. If I was very, very good
    I listened to "The Lone Ranger" with Tonto saving
    a farmer from bad men, BANG BANG.

Dad sang "I Love You Truly" and "Danny Boy"
    accompanying himself with this guitar. Mom's Irish
    eyes dancing, he wooed her again. How Jippy, our
    black cocker spaniel, howled when Dad reached
    for high notes, missing. Mom scowled;
    we made a beeline.

Mom used these curtain stretchers to do spring
    cleaning. Each year I set the stretchers on the
    lawn, reset them to catch the sun's rays,
    bleaching yellow lace white, whiter.

Down from the dark attic, out the screened window drifts
    a tenor's lullaby, putting a brown baby to sleep.

Monday

        is Wash Day. Water in the copper
boiler on the iron stove's front griddles finally
boils after armfuls of dry wood.

    I scoop pails of it, some for the Maytag
wringer machine, others for two set-tub rinses.
Cold spring water from the sink faucet lets
down the temperatures. Washing begins.

    Through the washer...wringer...rinse...
wringer...rinse...wringer...to the clothes
basket on the floor come first the white/light
colors. The dirtier/darker batches make
the water muddy, crunchy on the bottom.

    I hang sheets and pillowcases on the line
by the roadside; people passing won't see
underwear hidden near the house. Unionsuits
frozen stiff, ghostly creatures, collapse into
the clothes basket to finish drying over
the stove. Damp socks shrink on the oven door.

    Now the clothes basket holds shirts,
sheets, pants, pillowcases, washcloths,
dish towels, hand towels, handkerchiefs.
Tuesday is Ironing Day.

Catch the Grass

A scythe must   swing way back
and catch the   grass just so
to cut the best   or else the grass
      gets mangled.

The old fence line   requires a rhythm,
a romantic tune   that waltzes...
swish of skirts   as black-eyed Susans
      swoop

held just a second   in the scythe's embrace.
In morning dew   Susans wink no more;
the humble bee   finds sleepy lids
      remain.

Insects jump   before the scythe.
To cut its best   swing way back
and catch   the grass
      just so.

Hall Tree

Methodists supply a furnished
home for ministers. Our family
donates the scratchy old sofa
stuffed with horsehair, an area
rug, oak hall tree.
    On its arms we stored
    umbrellas, hats; wet
    overshoes, boots
    went into its seat.

Time passes; the minister rents
a home. I buy back the hall tree
for only a few hundred. Oak
stain covers its water marks,
umbrella scratches.
    The mirror reflects
    my white branches;
    marks, scratches
    hide inside my bark.

Reflections

Inga M. Potter

Dedicated to my daughter,
Shari L. Gaylord – best friend, best poetry critic,
in thanks for all the great years
and everything only you know how to give

Power

I'm mindful that the hibernating bears
do not rely on current for their heat
to insulate them in their winter lairs.
By nature, born unfurred, I'm incomplete
and therefore bought a blanket, white as snow.
I turn it up to "three" each gelid night,
anticipating comfort, for I know
that its electric heat will bring delight.
Those bears just slumber on till signs of spring;
warm and content, they doze without a care.
I'm toasty warm as well, but there's one thing
that worries me, while ice is in the air –
a rotted tree might topple on the line
and disconnect this white cocoon of mine!

Thai Woman

Thin black hair
is pulled back
from an amber face;

fine wisps float
along full cheeks.
Smiles crinkle her eyes

into ebony almonds.
Cream, blue and salmon
are woven into the shawl

that covers her shoulders.
It is her time to mother
the grandson who rides

in a wicker basket
on her back. Solemn-faced,
he holds her neck

with both hands. Slowly,
she walks home
from poetry class,

yearning to try
the old, formal style.
Words buzz in her head

as she composes a love poem
for the boy; a *Klon'pet ton*,
eight-line verse

in two stanzas.
She will surprise him,
when he has learned to read.

Night Music

Last night the winds of winter played a tune
whose eerie music filled my soul with dread.
Black silhouetted trees against the moon
threw long gyrating patterns on my bed.
As if a mad conductor took delight
in drawing forth cacophonies of notes,
he introduced sopranos of the night,
bewitching tunes from coyotes' lifted throats.
The music held me spellbound by its power,
and all of nature's orchestrated score
enchanted me for one inspired hour
of winter's wildness, with one last encore,
a repetitious melancholy howl –
the contrapuntal hooting of an owl.

Insight

She dropped her blue silk robe
and assumed a relaxed,
seated pose; chin on right hand,

left hand across her knees –
motionless, as though
cast in bronze. We could hardly wait

to squeeze oils on palettes,
grab brushes and try to capture
the magic of her sepia body.

Once she had modeled, well-paid,
for professional artists. Now
she sat for art school classes

for five dollars an hour.
She wove between our easels,
curious to see our attempts,

amateurish, but, because of her,
inspired. When she turned
her ebony eyes on my canvas,

I could tell, from her expression,
that she knew why I had outlined
her firm brown torso in royal blue.

Image of a Vanished Past

Photograph of a boy – Boston 1892

His solemn face looks straight at you.
A brimless hat perches, like a crown,
on thick, black hair.

Shirt buttons are gone, but two strings
fasten the wrinkled rag
across his thin chest.

A well-worn, unlined jacket is clutched,
like a sling, over his left shoulder.
A rope holds up his too-large trousers.

I am reminded of Michelangelo's David:
that same determined look,
stone-ready for Goliath.

Sisters

I stare at the bronze bust
Mother made of you
when you were eighteen,

capturing your beauty
for all time. I want to melt
your metal mouth

so we can talk, but you stare back,
silently, with vacant eyes.
Five years between us

were too many. I was an infant
when you left for school. Later
I followed, wearing your alpaca coat.

Adolescence found me in a dark pit.
You asked, "Ever had a French kiss?"
I lied. You should have told me everything.

You and father jabbered in Swedish
and barely noticed
me sitting beside you.

When I was older, I thought the gap
might close. Finally, we could talk.
But it was not to be.

I wrote my first poem that June night
a drunk driver
silenced your lips forever.

Autumn

Some picture Autumn in a man's attire.
To me, October's artisan is tall,
all feminine and zaftig, full of fire,
prepared to mesmerize us every fall.
Her time of year presented with great flair,
she spills her horn-of-plenty on the land
while moonlight sparkles on her russet hair.
Thus, while we sleep, with palette in her hand,
she paints the silent landscape, field and town,
with magic brushes carried in her sleeves.
She dances in her amber velvet gown,
incarnadining summer's waiting leaves.

As this astounding opulence appears,
she cleans her spattered hands for future years.

River's Edge

Sally Anne Reisner

Dedicated to my
husband Rich, the love of my life.
Let's grow old together.

Sally Anne Reisner

Sifting through Time

Nestled on the sofa in front of the fire
we sat side by side,
two sisters perusing pictures in the family albums,
searching for memories of our youth.

Look at that hair color! that style!
What were we thinking?
Look at that outfit!
Were we ever that young?

We turned back time, smiling and laughing
at the first formal, first high heels and
early childhood friends and sweethearts.
We felt a tender twining as we sifted
through shared familial heartaches,
separating good times from bad.

We knew what held the pages together.
It was simple.
We had been there for each other.

Always.

My Childhood Room

I remember being tucked in each night with whispers
of sweet dreams and forehead kisses,
snuggling in bed searching for shooting stars,
imagining shapes in the branches
of the giant evergreen tree outside my window.

I remember soft yellow wallpaper scattered
with tiny delicate flowers patterned like a patchwork quilt,
a dressing table with a white muslin skirt trimmed
with chenille balled fringe, Nana's sterling silver
hand-held mirror on top.

I remember a painted blue bookcase
in front of double windows with a dented
metal globe spinning next to my phonograph;
two closets full of white blouses, pleated skirts,
and my sister's hand-me-downs.

I remember feeling most complete when sitting at my desk,
with carved wooden scrolls and cubby holes
and a writing surface covered
with burnt red velveteen,
to write my poems upon.

On My Terms

You asked me to leave the bedroom,
but I wasn't ready.
I needed to prepare my space;
this was to be a step up, not out,
and it would be on my terms, not yours.

For twenty-four years we shared
that double bed,
that room with the slanted floor
and peeling wallpaper,
breakfast in bed looking through
diamond panes of leaded glass
at the changing colors
and falling leaves; it was
like living in a tree house.

I've redecorated the spare room with all that
I want: an antique desk and family
heirlooms. The new box spring and mattress
is covered with a patchwork quilt.
It's my room now.

As I lie in bed I feel
a renewed sense of solitude, of peace.
I cuddle under the ceiling stars,
remnants of our son's years in this room,
and look forward to a new day.

No more empty spaces,
echoes of silence
or antagonizing gloom.
No more false hopes.
No more lies.

I am ready.

The Old House:
Divisions of My Past and Present

The old house looks abandoned.
The moss covered roof sags with age and
scaffolding litters the lawn. Scattered cedar shakes
shine in the sunlight as I drive by.
Is anybody home?

I park the car and retrace my steps, tripping over gutters
collapsed and left to ruin.
I peek in windows and see wooden columns
dividing the dining room and living room, like
divisions of my past and present.

Could that room filled with dusty unfinished furniture
be the same room where we had Thanksgiving dinners
with parents since deceased?
Could that living room filled with piles of rags and stacks of
magazines be where Christmas trees stood year after year?

Laundry hangs from beams in the old farmhouse kitchen
where crisp dried flowers once hung. The bake oven is filled
with rusty coffee cans where dark bread baked beside the
open hearth. An old wood stove stands where fires once blazed
and children's winter jackets were left to dry.

Mother's Day

Hanging laundry on the line,
tasting the wind on my face,
I look upward at the greening trees.
The shirts and shorts form a parenthesis
with my stretching body
as I connect each wooden clothespin.

How can I feel so content
on Mother's Day
with my sons so far away?

Then the phone rings.
Happy Mother's Day, Mom. I love you.
I love you, too, sweetheart.
The miles vanish.

Later, with the turkey in the oven
and the laundry folded, the phone rings again.
... I love you, too, son. I'm proud of you both.
We're proud of you, Mom.

My two sons,
both sides of the parentheses,
with me in the middle.
We're connected
no matter how far apart.

Morning Chorus

Early morning dawned as I crept quietly
from our summer bedroom to begin my daily ritual
of inspecting the garden.

What needs to be snipped?
What needs to be watered?
What can be added to my tabletop bouquet?

Last night as I gazed at the flowers
in the moonlight
all was calm; all was still.

Yet, this morning something has trumpeted a change.

There, amidst the delphinium and coreopsis,
hiding behind the hollyhocks and Asiatic lilies
are musical notes.

Some stand solitary.
Others cluster in a chorus.
Dainty, silvery musical notes, almost iridescent.

I sing in wonder, joining
the capped choir of fleshy fungi!

Don't Leave Me

Moonlight filtered through the summer screens
lights your face with a soft lens.
Your head rests peacefully on the dampened pillowcase
as I caress your body gently, the light touch of a feather.
Your porcelain skin alarms me.
Don't leave me, dear friend.

Visions of past joys parade through my mind:
our wedding in the park, with the children beside us;
the honeymoon in Paris; the opera in Verona under the stars;
champagne in our hot tub, looking at the skyline;
the fiords of Norway, waterfalls around every turn;
the Portuguese countryside; tastings at the Institute of Port.

It's so peaceful living here in Vermont
in our log cabin in the woods.
How can this be?
We embrace each day with faith,
each night with a reassuring calm.
Stay with me, sweetheart.

Beneath the Surface

Dorothy M. Warren

in memory of my parents
Mary Lees and Thomas Edgar Warren

Communing

Before yellow buses,
Dad drove me to high school every day.
We didn't speak much.

I was a self conscious teenager.
He was not one to probe
my secret thoughts.

Instead, we whistled on the ten mile trip,
mainly Gilbert and Sullivan ballads
or patriotic nonsense songs.

My grandmother warned about "whistling maids
and crowing hens." I matured away at college
and far from home – too late.

His was a short life. I regret
having stayed young so long, unable to talk,
as one adult to another.

Now, when whistling at chores,
I see his profile, two hands on the wheel,
driving me through time with love.

Daily Ritual

Down the winding drive
she strolls
with a straight back
that belies
her eighty-seven years.
Past giant pines
her husband planted,
past old cherry trees
she walks,
breathing in
sweet-smelling
lilies of the valley.
She crosses
the road with caution
to her battered mailbox,
waves to a friendly neighbor,
then makes her way back
with lively step,
letter in hand.

Double Feature

When I was nine, Saturday was a big day.

Mary Morton and I would head into her father's diner,
    past the pinball machine
    where hockey players skated forever,
    past the lunch counter reeking of onions,
    right up to the cash register
    where Mary got her weekly allowance.

With cash in pocket, we'd hurry to the Granada,
    a small-town cinema less chic than others,
    mainly because its Saturday clientele
    was totally comprised of under twelve-year-olds.
    The seats were worn;
    their backs bore the imprint of many shoes.
    Candy wrappers and popcorn cluttered the floor.

Oblivious to our decadent surroundings,
    we reveled in the exploits of Zorro,
    cried when Lassie was in trouble,
    hid our eyes during Frankenstein.
    It didn't matter when we went in.
    We often sat through a second show
    to catch the part missed in the first.

With credits running on the screen,
    we'd meander out with the crowd,
    then dawdle back home hand-in-hand,
    retelling the adventures just seen.
    We'd praise the bravado of handsome movie stars,
    and speculate on events to unfold.

No two fourth graders ever felt more blissful.

Grace Notes

Years ago,
my cousins set out
from Ontario for the West Coast,
in an old truck piled high
with children and furniture.

The Rockies
proved to be a big hurdle.
Here, like a sinking rowboat,
their truck had to be made lighter
to climb the mountains.

First went the heavy books
into a chasm,
then their old iron bedstead
and finally the antique piano
brought by my grandparents from England.

Down it crashed,
smashing past pines and rock,
startling grazing mountain sheep,
to lodge without ceremony
in that cemetery of debris.

But I like to think that the inglorious fall
of a once-fine instrument
was redeemed by little creatures
tickling the ivory keys,
producing strange echoes off canyon walls.

Dorothy M. Warren

As Seen from Route 100

Among knee-high weeds,
its walls sag
under a rusty roof.

Imitation brick siding
offers a vain attempt
to keep up appearances,
but rotting clapboards
refuse
to support the pretense.

Its proximity to the road
is temptation
for stone-throwing boys;
black, broken window panes
welcome the wind and rain.

Empty within,
this gray-brown skeleton
once housed a farmer's family.
Shouts of children chasing chickens
used to mix
with the roar of the tractor.

Now,
from the deserted house,
a single lace curtain
waves in silence.

Horse and Train

Oil painting by Alex Colville

Riderless,
with all hooves in air,
a stallion gallops
over railroad ties
toward infinity.

He races, mesmerized
by the shine
of two, white-hot rails
and the spell of the light
from an on-coming train.

He charges
to meet his nemesis –
head-on.
The closer he gets,
the brighter the light
and the surer his fate.

On either side,
the flat, barren landscape
stretches,
sinister and calm,
oblivious
to impending
disaster.

Vanitas Vanitatum

I fought with my brother
to gain the golden throne,
to wear the royal asp,
to keep from delivering the wealth of Egypt
into the Roman grasp.

When Caesar arrived to restore order,
my trusted slave presented me
wrapped in a carpet – gold bordered,
as befitted my beauty
and a dramatic entrance.

I seduced the aging warrior
who gladly crowned me queen,
admiring my youthful body –
also my head filled with ambitious plans
and schemes.

But my triumph was brief;
with Caesar's murder, I was alone
to protect our son,
to defend my throne –
until Marc Antony strode ashore.

I welcomed him with ceremony
that out-orgied his Roman feasting.
Again my charms worked well,
and love we did,
until the conquering Octavian broke the spell.

Now, in this treasure-filled tomb,
defeated in battle, with Antony dead,
I refuse humiliation that awaits in Rome.
I proudly submit to death by my own hand;
the serpent is quick.

)

Floating

Jane Stewart Wollmar

Dedicated to my mother Margaret Ritchie Stewart
who passed on her love of language and literature
and
my husband Stellan
whose artistic abilities and appreciation
surround and sustain me.

Merging

As far as you can look,
you cannot tell
where sky ends
and sea begins.

A vast blueness
surrounds
white billows.

You fly in the ocean,
gliding.
You swim in the sky,
stroking.

Riding a wave,
catching a current.

There is no rightside up.

Stay Tuned

In memory of Alan Stewart
November 5, 1903 - October 13, 2000

You were so mighty a presence.
Now your ashes
are covered with snow,
but your essence is
like surround sound.
The waves are there;
it just takes tuning in.

You are an equally mighty absence.
Occasionally I sense a surge,
many hours just a hum,
and now and then,
to receive you,
I have to pause
and finely adjust my dials.

Island Blues

I get the blues in Nevis:

Aquamarine shallows dissolve
into indigo depths.
The distant cobalt sea rises
in white foaming wavelets,
while pale azure
stretches
even the clouds
across the sky.

I get the blues in Nevis:

Progressive harmonies
of wind in palms and
rhythmic breaking surf
are accented by bleats of baby goats
and squeaks of banana kwits.
Monkeys improvise
in syncopated chatter,
scat-singing with braying burros.

I get the blues in Nevis:

My spirit colors;
my soul sings.

Keeping Track

This crisp winter morning,
armed with tracking specs,
I snowshoe through
the forest transect.

I pass beech trees
scarred with
claw and teeth marks
of black bears.

Hemlocks and spruce
shelter the deer yard,
stamped-down snow
and hollows melted
by warm doe bodies.

I follow the tiny mounded
tunnel of a mole
who prefers to travel
under the white safety net.

My steps match long leaps
of a snowshoe hare,
fleeing a fox
whose bushy tail drags
as a fifth paw
across the white slate.

Curl-ended scat
full of silver gray fur shows
coyotes are finding food
in this essential habitat.

Going All the Way

At the beach at Nauset
I court the breakers
and beyond,
always needing
to go the farthest.

My parents frantically
signal me back,
but I never mind,
ignoring them in my
adolescent omnipotence.

Until the whistle.
The tanned guard
in his fluorescent suit
stands on his eight foot chair
and waves me in.

Embarrassed, I come in,
just so far,
still flirting
with that fine line
that tempts teenagers:

How far can I go?

Picture Show

Through two large frames,
I view the show,
playing in slowest motion.

Glistening, glass-coated
gray-brown boughs
fill the screen.

As the plot unfolds,
the branches assume
a pale mauve aura;
the tint changes
to bright chartreuse.

At the climax,
rich green foliage
patched with blue
is intensified by
playing light and shadows.

The shot of a single
yellow leaf evolves
into a panorama of
glorious golden
technicolor.

The falling action continues;
as leaves drop,
more neutral bare limbs
and sky are revealed.
Denouement.

Without intermission,
the next picture show begins.
I never tire of the story.

Grandchild

I take the dare.
"Oh, GranJane,
you must be a city girl;
country girls dive off the rocks!"
She is faster in backstroke than I,
but I can get across the pond first
in freestyle, holding nothing back
to graciously let the child win.
Afterwards we sit on the hot rocks,
debating who has the better life:
mermaid-she or land-lady-me.

We play old rock and roll,
familiar now to her in its
second time around.
Dancing to *Rockin' Robin,*
she's as amazed by my moves
as I am by hers.
"Cool," she admires.

She shops with me,
posing in four-inch wedge shoes,
while I slant the brim
of a chartreuse hat
with gigantic red poppy.
"Gorgeous, dahling," she giggles.

After dessert of her-made brownies,
we pile pillows and quilts
to sleep out on the deck.
Lying awake under the stars,
she makes a wish.
I have my wish:
this granddaughter
and my youth again.

Born in 1947, **Carol Collins** was raised on a sheep farm in Brattleboro, Vermont. In 1972 she and husband Fred built their home in Duxbury and raised Seth and Eliza. She taught high school creative writing and now operates her spinning business – Singing Spindle Spinnery – which she founded in 1982. Writing poetry since age five, Carol does poetry readings, workshops, editing and has published in several literary publications. She is an accomplished photographer whose work has appeared in several exhibitions.

Putting words to paper has been a lifelong avocation for **Ann Day**. Her first published poem was in a summer camp newspaper in 1936. In 1954 she moved with her husband and two children to the Mad River Valley. She has been *The Valley Reporter's* nature columnist for over thirty years and has traveled New England with her poetry slide program. To share her curiosity and caring for the natural world has been a passion that has motivated Ann all her life.

Earline Marsh, a lifelong dabbler in poetry, recently became a dedicated poet. As a teacher, principal and school volunteer over the years, she has encouraged young people to read and write poetry. She serves as an on-line mentor to student poets, as part of the Vermont Poetry Project. Earline is a hand papermaker who teaches this ancient craft in her new studio in a mid-nineteenth century barn in Moretown, Vermont.

After teaching high school in a suburb of New York City, **Carol Milkuhn** retired to Vermont where she has discovered a second career in writing poetry. She thanks Peggy Montgomery and Mickey Henriquez for reading her endless drafts, Joan Austin, Tanya Hawk, Joan Renke and Julie Pease for their encouragement and support, and Gil Freeman for his generosity in sharing his account of volunteer work at Ground Zero.

Ruth Pestle is Professor Emerita of Family and Consumer Sciences Education at Florida State University. She authored research articles, "A Heritage to Remember and Share: The Family and Consumer Sciences Education Association 1927-2002," and a chap book of poetry, "Remembrances." Now Ruth travels, studies, assists the

Waitsfield Historical Society and The Poetry Society of Vermont, and tends her flower gardens in Florida and Vermont. She enjoys the beauty of this world, its people, and her time in it.

Inga Potter is the youngest of three children of immigrant Swedish-Americans; both her mother and uncle were poets. Her love of oil painting also came from her mother, who was an artist and sculptress. She started writing poetry in 1976 as a new member of The Poetry Society of Vermont. She self-publisheh a chap book, "Poems and Sketches," in 1996.

Sally Anne Reisner grew up in the San Francisco Bay Area in the fifties. She attended college in the East and then taught in an urban-suburban high school in New Jersey for eighteen years. At the age of fifty she left her job, remarried and focused on her writing. She enjoys giving writing workshops for teachers and is an online mentor to young poets. She and her husband currently live in a log home in Fayston, Vermont.

Dorothy M. Warren was born in Hamilton, Ontario. She is a graduate of Syracuse University (Fine Arts) and McMaster University (English) in Hamilton. She has been a painter of watercolors and oils for many years, exhibiting in group and solo shows. A longtime middle school teacher of art and English literature in Canada, she now lives in Warren, Vermont with her husband John G. Hutton, Jr., to whom she dedicates her poetry.

"I have a little shadow..." is **Jane Stewart Wollmar's** early memory of her mother reciting poetry. Jane became committed to studying and writing poetry at Goucher College under Sara DeFord. Initially an editor in a New York publishing company, Jane began teaching in 1983; she is a fellow of the National Writing Project in Connecticut which has had a major impact on her writing and teaching. Jane is currently a special educator and President of The Poetry Society of Vermont.

All nine Mad River Poets are also active members of
The Poetry Society of Vermont.

To order copies of this book, send your name, address, and a check for $15.95 (the price of the book plus $3.00 for shipping and handling) to:

The Mad River Poets
P.O. Box 1299
Waitsfield, VT 05673

Vermont residents add 5% (65¢) sales tax.